ISBN: 979-8-9879928-1-4

(CC) Adam Draper. Some rights reserved under the Creative Commons Attribution-ShareAlike License 3.0 (CC-BY-SA)

To Andrea, my wife,
who has gifted me infinite luck.
To my Mom, who raised
four children with conviction.
To my Grandmother, who loved writing.
To Pops, who this was written for.

BREAKFAST WITH POPS

A Venture Capital Handbook

Adam Draper & William Henry Draper, III

www.breakfastwithpops.com

Table of Contents

Introduction
Welcome to Breakfast 1

Chapter 1
A Brief & Incomplete History of Venture Capital 11

Chapter 2
VC in 5 Words 29

Chapter 3
People 31

Chapter 4
Lifestyle 73

Chapter 5
Trust   79

Chapter 6
Conviction   89

Chapter 7
Luck   105

Chapter 8
Things I Say to Founders   111

Glossary of Startup Lingo   118

Welcome to Breakfast

Every two weeks for the last 5 years, I've had breakfast with my grandfather Bill Draper. I call him Pops. Some people call him a legend. This handbook is my attempt to distill the knowledge of venture capital he's passed down over eggs and bacon in the 100+ breakfasts we've enjoyed together.

I got into venture capital the old-fashioned way. My great-grandfather founded it, my grandfather improved on it, and my dad took it global. My family's history is synonymous with the history of venture capital in Silicon Valley—it's hard to talk about VC in the last 70 years and not mention "the Drapers."

As a result, I know venture capitalism the way a cobbler's son knows cobbling. It's the trade/craft that my dad, granddad, and great-granddad all chose to pursue; I was their apprentice, and I'm now a VC too.

I'm proud of that and grateful for it. I started with a leg up on the average new venture capitalist, being raised with stories of the founding of Tesla, Hotmail and Skype. Our dinner table conversations were always about cool ideas and technologies that scale.

With that knowledge, I founded Boost VC, became the first investor in Coinbase, and invested in 400+ startups in my first 12 years as an investor. I've written either the first or second check to 7 companies that reached billion-dollar valuations, back when they were two- or three-person teams. And our first fund at Boost returned more capital than 95% of funds that year.

My unique history with this industry got me thinking: **How can I give this experience to someone else?** How can I start to share what I've learned?

Breakfast With Pops is my first attempt to put the most important knowledge into one place. The main character is my grandfather, a.k.a. Pops, a.k.a. William Henry Draper III. He's the most charming man you could meet, and he's still sharper than everyone.

Buck's

Breakfast is at Buck's restaurant in Woodside, CA. It's a family restaurant with a secret: VCs have invested in some of the greatest startups in history at these tables. Rumor has it that the Google and Yahoo deals were both put together here. There are a couple of little clues, like the display case labeled "Thanks for the memories!" containing a collection of silicon memory chips made over many years. But there's also a hanging model airplane and one of Shaquille O'Neal's basketball shoes.

During one of our breakfasts, if someone were to look at us directly from the side, it would be like looking at a 90-year-old hanging out with his 30-year-old self, discussing business, politics and family. We do have a lot in common—except I'm wearing bright orange pants, while Pops is always dressed immaculately in a colorful collared shirt and a sport coat. (One time years ago, he wore this same outfit on a canoe trip, the canoe capsized and flipped him into the water, and, I swear to you, he walked out of the water with the sport coat tossed over his shoulder, looking like Sean Connery in James Bond. He didn't look wet. He was completely unshaken, with a grin on his face).

To this day, when I look at Pops, I see the grace of 50 kings rolled into the 6-foot frame of an athletic 90-year-old, although he claims to be shrinking. He still wakes up and uses his stationary bike for 30 minutes before he starts his day.

In 1965, Pops founded Sutter Hill Ventures, where he and his team funded hundreds of early-stage, high-tech companies making semiconductors, defibrillators, copy machines, operating systems, etc.

From 1981 to 1986, he left VC to serve as the Chairman of the Export-Import Bank of the U.S., upon the request of Ronald Reagan. He then jumped over to being Under-Secretary General of the United Nations, where he ran the United Nations Development program and got to visit 110 countries to aid in their development. In 1994, he co-founded Draper International, the first U.S.

venture capital fund to focus on investing in private companies with operations in India. In 2002, he co-founded Draper Richards LP, which invests in American early-stage tech companies, and he also founded Draper Investment Company, which concentrates on seed investments in Europe and Asia. Finally, he co-founded the Draper Richards Kaplan Foundation, the first "Social Entrepreneurship fund," which backs nonprofits like they're startups.

Today, people I've never met before sometimes tell me, "Your grandfather was such a great mentor to me!"

I've learned from hundreds of breakfasts with Pops that change is a constant, but core values are unstoppable. Even in the fast, ever-changing world of technology, some things don't change. Pops has dropped the most amazing knowledge bombs on me (and many other people), particularly drilling down on the core elements that make up venture capital investing.

We both hope this handbook helps people who are starting out in early-stage VC: new angel investors, associates at venture funds, and all others who've found themselves holding what Pops always calls "the best job in the world."

Chapter 1
A BRIEF & INCOMPLETE HISTORY OF VENTURE CAPITAL

Before we discuss the unchanging truths of venture capital over pancakes, let's see what **HAS** changed.

Today, investors can shop around for entrepreneurs online and vice versa. But from the 1950s through the early 2000s, VC was a game of access. There were a small number of venture capitalists who'd share whatever deals they managed to find.

Pops tells stories of driving up and down "the orchards" of Silicon Valley in the 1960s, trying to find any office that had a sign that said TECHNOLOGY on the front.

He'd knock on the door and say, "I'm a venture capitalist. Can I speak with the president of this company?"

They'd push back and ask, "What's an adventure capitalist?"

But once they understood that he had money and wanted to invest in their business, they'd usher him into a meeting with their president.

Early Prototypes of VC

The spirit of early-stage venture capital is centuries old. But initially, governments had a monopoly on funding new breakthrough technologies and discoveries: think of Queen Isabella funding Christopher Columbus' quest for a new passage to India, or Genghis Khan funding the production of better military gear.

Things started changing around 1900. When Pops talks about the "ancient history" of venture, he goes back to the 1930s. At that time, a few companies started doing something that looked like modern venture capital, without using that phrase. These were family offices belonging to wealthy East Coasters, including the Whitneys and Rockefellers. These families had started to throw their weight behind potentially high-reward investments that banks and governments wouldn't touch. They figured out that the biggest gains came from supporting early-stage investments in companies that hadn't gone public yet, like Minute Maid and Eastern Air Lines.

This was the breakthrough innovation of venture capital: backing scalable businesses as a small, independent group. Venture capital is a way to fund innovation outside of the incentive structure of governments and corporations. Now, smaller businesses had capital to pursue incredible breakthroughs.

LP + GP Structure

In 1959, my great-grandfather, William Henry Draper Jr., started Draper, Gaither & Anderson (DGA) after a decorated military career. He ended up in California without much money—he certainly didn't have enough to start a family office like the Rockefellers'. But he was into the idea of venture capital. Being near Stanford, with all those young people full of energy, inspired him to invest in their ideas.

DGA was the first venture capital company in the world that was founded with the model which is standard today: a partnership with Limited Partners (LPs) and General Partners (GPs).

The model is super simple: the General Partners manage the Limited Partners' money. The GPs steward the capital day to day. They have an incentive to make it grow: they get paid some money annually based on the money committed by LPs, and then get paid a larger percentage if they return all the capital and more!

My great-grandfather and the other general partners at DGA raised $6 million from a handful of LPs who had money (including, weirdly enough, the Rockefellers). They reserved a 2.5% management fee ($150,000) to pay their overhead and promised 60% of any profits to their LPs. The other 40% of profits was called the "carry," which the general partners would split among themselves.

Thousands of VC firms around the world now use this structure, with varying percentages for the management fee and the carry. (Now the carry is more often 20%, and the management fee is 2%).

Sutter Hill Ventures

In 1964, Pops took the VC torch from my great-grandfather by starting Sutter Hill Ventures. The business of venture was still small in the eyes of the money management industry as a whole, but the investments performed well.

Pops talks about deals in those days as if they were all handshakes.

"Today, it's completely different," he says. "Back then, we'd say 'You're putting in the blood, sweat and hard work, and we're putting up the capital, so how about we partner 50/50?'"

Through Sutter Hill Ventures, Pops became an investor in early copy machines, the first defibrillator, and early computer companies. These breakthroughs changed the world.

Attention From Wall Street in the 1970s

In the 1960s, a lot of term sheets (non-binding agreements showing the basic terms and conditions of an investment) were still drafted on napkins. Now we have 3x preferences, pro rata, and board seats.

If you ask Pops about these changes, he'll say, "I knew that the industry was going to change when the Goldman Sachs CEO was in my office."

Pops is saying that in the beginning, Wall Street investors ignored him and his friends. But then the East Coast financiers caught wind of the ~40% returns these West Coasters were earning. Wall Street was still chasing single digits.

After sniffing around Pops' office, they unloaded as much of their capital as they could into startups, chasing those massive returns. In doing that, they bent financial history towards innovation and Silicon Valley.

Pops says, "After our meeting, the Goldman Sachs CEO went back to New York, filled a truck with cash, drove it to Silicon Valley, and dumped it."

Because of this, and subsequent legal changes to allow pension funds to invest in venture capital, the scale of the money in VC had changed. This led to a more competitive industry.

Going Global in the '90s and 2000s

In the early 1990s, venture capital had been focused on the United States. But the enormous growth of this new "Internet" technology started to attract builders from all over the world. My Dad was well positioned for this, as he'd started his own VC firm—Draper Fisher Jurvetson (DFJ)—in 1985. DFJ was the first fund to raise an "Internet investment" fund, which attracted some bold, forward-thinking LPs with the foresight to invest specifically in Internet-related opportunities.

VC was on the cusp of going global. Through 1999, off of the success of companies like Hotmail (Sold to Microsoft), and 411.com (Sold to Yahoo), my Dad recognized that entrepreneurs were everywhere. At that point, DFJ was able to raise a global investment fund, the first of its kind, called DFJ ePlanet.

Soon VC opened up beyond the West Coast and the US, to the whole world. After all, great technology was being built all over the world, and investors everywhere wanted the economic upside. My Dad launched the global DFJ Network as a franchise play on VC, becoming the first venture fund in more than 27 countries. This network invested in many international ventures, including Skype and Baidu. In parallel, my grandfather founded the first venture fund in India and returned 16x with his partner Robin Richards.

It's a sharp contrast to the hyper-local beginnings of the business, when it took years for Wall Street to even notice what venture capitalists were doing. This explosive growth around the turn of the Millennium caused even more capital to pour into the venture industry, not only from Wall Street but from everywhere in the world.

Y Combinator (2005)

~50 years in, Silicon Valley was a powerhouse driven in large part by the network of students at Stanford, Hewlett Packard, Silicon Graphics, and Intel. For decades, every startup was rooted in the Stanford network. But a change started to brew in the mid-2000s.

The typical venture deal in 2005 looked radically different from the model Pops had used in the '60s. Competition and the scale of the dollars in venture capital had changed the stakes and the game. Deals were more standardized. Many clauses of these new contracts were about protecting people from downside, not just sharing upside.

Starting a technology startup had also gotten much cheaper. No one needed servers anymore; any 16-year-old with a laptop could start the next billion-dollar business over the Internet... with as little as $15k.

Paul Graham, Jessica Livingston, Trevor Blackwell and Robert Morris saw this coming and started Y Combinator. They rejected the standardized "best practices" that had started to weigh down the venture model.

Before Y Combinator, you couldn't invest in more than 20 companies per fund, and a $15,000 investment was too small to be worthwhile. But Y Combinator wrote checks in unexpected amounts, including $15,000, because there were people (college students) who were ready and able to build from there.

Y Combinator reduced the cost of starting a company by flipping the model: they took equity for a small investment, and gave startups the resources and focus to pitch more investors at the end of their 3-month program. Y Combinator timed this movement perfectly with how cheap it had become to build for the Internet. Y Combinator describes companies like AirBnB, Stripe, DropBox, Coinbase and Benchling as "alumni."

Today, Y Combinator invests in more companies every year than most funds have ever backed. The most recent batch had 250+ startups, and they do that twice a year. They have become the most powerful network in startup history in 15 years. Their innovations inspired me to start Boost VC with a similar model.

Y Combinator created new deal standards that shifted the balance of power in the direction of the founder. One of their most underestimated creations is the SAFE investment standard (Simple Agreement for Future Equity). SAFE allows startups to receive funding before the shares are valued formally.

Post Financial Crisis (2009 and Beyond)

In the most recent decade, venture capital has become a household name. Very few companies have reached a billion-dollar valuation without VC funding. We've seen new changes and innovations:

- Y Combinator began to flourish and grow from 10 deals in their first batch to 250+ in their 2022 group.

- AngelList, founded by Naval Ravikant and Babak Nivi, created a network where you can browse startups that are fundraising online.

- Carta aggregated everyone's capitalization tables, and now has the best data set on venture capital investors in the world.

- A16Z scaled their fund size to tens of billions of dollars and paved the way for more MEGA funds.

- From Bitcoin to DAOs, we continue to experiment with new ways to fund breakthroughs globally.

You can fund and run a company in ways Pops could never have imagined when he started in this business.

In the future, I think VC will continue to expand, playing out on a bigger field with many more players. Future VC might look different, just as today's VC looks different from those early family offices. **But there are 5 elemental concepts which I'm convinced aren't going to change.** That's what we'll talk about from here on.

Chapter 2
VC IN 5 WORDS

This is the list of what hasn't changed in venture capital.

People.

Lifestyle.

Trust.

Conviction.

Luck.

Chapter 3
PEOPLE

Buck's is always fast to get you coffee. I asked for cold brew the first 20 times I went, and slowly realized I wouldn't change this historic institution with my new-aged coffee needs. Pops and I both get hot, black coffee. He follows it up with a glass of orange juice.

I once asked Pops about the SINGLE MOST IMPORTANT THING in venture capital.

Here's what he said:

It's a people business. It's backing the right people and not the wrong people. Get to know the people you're backing really well.

If you aren't good at people, you should be in another business.

If you're good at people, it will make you very successful, and you'll make lots of friends and money. People are the heart of the whole business.

People often forget that people build the technology you use. That's why the technology business isn't just about technology. It's about the people who decide to go out and build it, deliver it to a store, and make it possible for you to buy it. People are the heart of the business of capital.

Your network is paramount in this business. Your network is the list of people you'd be willing to introduce to a friend. It's also the number of people you know who could help the average startup.

Fortunately, if you're a people person, *you've already built an amazing network.* You've made connections in school, sports, business, and life. You've met dynamic and unforgettable people. Maybe your network is specialized in a niche like healthcare, consumer products, aerospace or crypto. Keep being a people person. **Your best deals could already be in front of you, in the form of people you know.**

And then, become more proactive than ever in your network building. This is the fun part!

A few timeless networking tactics:

- Meet 4 new people every day.
- Say yes to all meetings in your first few years.
- Reach out to people you've always wanted to meet.
- Be fearless.
- Create a system for trying things, making mistakes, and moving on.
- Help anyone you can help.

Partnerships

Families are partnerships. Businesses are partnerships. Friendships are partnerships.

When I married my wife, Andrea, Pops said, "Well, you made one good decision, and that was the most important one you can make. Everything else is just details." He was married to my grandmother, Phyllis Draper, for 60 years.

VC has a lot in common with marriage. Venture capital investments last longer than most marriages! It's about finding the right people, sparking a relationship, and nurturing it into an unbreakable partnership.

It takes courage to commit. It takes a desire to be better. It takes energy to build. A great partnership is one in which trust is absolute. When you get it right, luck has a way of presenting itself repeatedly.

After we've both drained our coffee and our bellies are full of bacon, Pops gets incredibly animated. He loves talking about the people he's chosen to partner with.

He tells a good story about how he met his partner, Robin Richards, for Draper International. They made the decision after one 3-hour brunch, and their powerful partnership lasted more than 20 years.

It started in 1994. Pops was talking to his friend Bill McGlashan. Pops expressed his desire to invest in the developing world.

Bill brought Pops to Stanford to meet a handful of business school students who were giving a presentation about investment opportunities in Chile. One of those students was Robin Richards. Pops remembers noticing her competence in that context, but he left the room without thinking much more of it.

A week later his fax machine spat out a sheet of paper that read:

Hi. I would like to talk to you about venture capital. Robin.

Pops was pleasantly surprised. Apparently he'd scribbled down his new fax number on a business card and given it to Robin. They met for breakfast that Saturday.

"I've never been more certain about my instinct than I was over breakfast that morning," Pops wrote. "She was *sharp*. In our three-hour mutual interview, the power of her big brain became more and more evident to me. This kind of brainpower is a blessing and goes a long way toward qualifying a person to be an extraordinary partner in a venture capital company. In addition, Robin had the gift of warmth and sensitivity as part of her exceptionally appealing personality. At our breakfast—and over the subsequent years—

I rarely heard her make a suggestion to me or anyone else without saying 'If you don't mind,' or adding, 'Assuming it's okay with you.' She always gives others the chance to talk, give opinions, or disagree… sensitivity and the ability to listen are terribly important to the venture capitalist."

Years later, Pops connected me with Robin Richards. I pitched Boost VC to her, hoping she'd join as a Limited Partner. And she expressed the most powerful sentiment I feel you can have toward a partner:

"I was so lucky to have ever crossed paths with Bill Draper."

I aspire to give people that feeling.

Brayton Williams, now my partner of 10+ years, first appeared during a double date at

P.F. Chang's. At the time I was working for a company I co-founded called Xpert Financial, a secondary market for private securities. After a short dinner we ended up hiring him as an analyst. He was the hardest worker at the company.

Brayton was my height with fluffy blonde hair. He had massive pectoral muscles when he started at Xpert, like a comic book superhero. But over time, he started looking more like a mere mortal.

After 18 months at Xpert Financial, we hadn't found our path to profitability, and we were spending too much. I had to lay off a lot of people, including Brayton.

He left... and then showed up for work the next day. And the day after that. And the day after that.

Eventually, he explained: "Well, I have nowhere else to be."

He worked just as hard as before, if not harder, helping us solve problems without being paid.

In response I pulled Brayton into my office and asked him if he wanted to start something new with me. He joined me enthusiastically, not knowing it would be a 10+ year journey and adventure.

Brayton and I are as different as two people can be (even though we both play as Ness in Super Smash Brothers). But we complement each other. We both tell people that if I were solo, I'd get nowhere, but if he were solo, he'd never get started.

It's true that I'd get nowhere without Brayton. He's great at the things I suck at, like tracking metrics and doing year-end reviews. He's got a cool head and is an assassin when it comes to operations. And I bring what Brayton (and others) have called "Draper optimism": willingness to stand up and do things that other people think are crazy, and to stand by founders who are doing crazy things.

I've been very lucky in life and love—I've been able to build partnerships with great people. I wish you the best of luck in finding the right partnerships for yourself. There's nothing more rewarding.

Limited Partners (LPs)

LPs are the people with money standing behind every venture fund. The "Limited" part is a misnomer. It trivializes the relationship between you and your funding partners. They should be called *unlimited* partners.

LPs are the brave few who invest alongside your decisions. They partner their capital with yours in order to make money, and they believe in your decision-making ability.

The partnership is what matters. You're trying to find partnership, not transactional money. (In macro good times, people tend to want a more transactional relationship, and in harder times a closer peer relationship).

In 2016, I was in the middle of a brutal fundraise for Boost VC: I was attempting to raise a $40M fund for crypto and VR. No one wanted to touch either technology. A very prominent endowment actually ended a meeting with me after 10 minutes, even though 1 hour had been scheduled.

I went to Pops for perspective. He asked me how many investors I'd spoken with. I took it on as a challenge—as if he didn't think I was doing the work—and pushed back, almost bragging: "I have spoken to 320 LPs!"

He said one sentence that changed my whole fundraising outlook from that moment on:

"320, and it's still not closed? ... **Maybe you're doing it wrong.**"

And just like that, he changed my perspective (and deflated my ego 😊). I'd been trying to break down a stone wall for 8 months, when there had been a door right next to it.

I had thought it was about the grind, selling and convincing. Pops opened the door to a different world—one where you just target the people who are already interested. I now think about LPs in a completely different way compared to when I first started (and I wish I'd figured this stuff out sooner, because it kept me up at night for a long time).

That's what we'll talk about next.

Fundraising from LPs

You know, during these breakfasts, I have a hard time believing my grandfather ever struggled with fundraising like I did. He's a master of people. During practically every meal at Buck's, multiple people will come over to him—everyone from the owner of the restaurant to founders he met decades ago.

It took me a while to understand: the point of the partnership between LPs and VCs is to solve a translation problem. The problem involves two groups of people.

1. LPs (people with a surplus of capital).

2. Entrepreneurs (people with a surplus of human endeavor).

You're the middleman, the marketplace; you're living between those who have too much capital to deploy by themselves and those who require capital to build. You get to be their matchmaker.

The hardest thing to realize when you're fundraising is *LPs just want you to solve their problem.* They don't care how it gets solved. That's your job. They want the confidence that you will solve it. Generally you should know: LPs don't want to do your job.

This was surprising to me because I couldn't imagine anyone not wanting to do my job. I have the best job in the world! I thought everyone saw my job as the fun part. But most LPs just want you to solve a problem in their asset allocation.

My mistake was trying to convince LPs of the value of an industry—like Bitcoin, VR, or Aerospace. But all that selling was wasted breath. **LPs have already decided to invest in an industry. By the time they meet you, they're assessing whether they think you are the right fit.**

Every LP meeting fits one of these descriptions:

1. They like YOU, so they're interested in allocating to you (or VC as a whole).

2. They like the market you're allocating to, and trust the person who referred you.

3. They're educating themselves on the topic to build conviction.

Maybe they already favor the general direction of crypto, gaming, defense tech, climate tech, medical devices, or whatever. Maybe they think you're good at picking good people in good industries. Either way, you won't do anyone any good trying to sell your industry or niche to LPs. It's more useful to describe to LPs why you are the best investor within that industry.

I think the best way to sum it up is the way my nonprofit friend talks about his industry. He says, "People will part with their money for only two reasons: it's something they care about, or the opportunity is referred to them by someone they trust."

Ideally, with LPs, you have both. You have a niche they care about, and you're someone they trust. This is why **it's important to specialize** in a niche of some sort. This is triple-true when you're early in your VC career. Otherwise, you have no track record—so it's hard to trust you—and you also aren't offering something specific for the LP to care about. After you have some experience, it's possible to broaden your scope because you'll have already established some trust. But even then, being a generalist is opening yourself up to needless competition. Both

LPs and founders want specialists more than generalists.

Note: *You may not be required to fundraise from Limited Partners if you join a fund that is well established and has consistent LPs already. But respect that someone in your organization was tasked with that role and built up an incredible amount of trust over years. You should probably search for the person who did it and thank them multiple times. Also remember, going through the process of fundraising is the clearest way to empathize with the founder's journey.*

Managing LPs After They've Invested

Once you've raised capital, your job with LPs is to **build an enduring partnership.** Consider it a long-term relationship, and they'll think the same.

Over-communication is good, especially with LPs. I've been sending either monthly or quarterly updates for 10 years, and my investors appreciate it because they feel included in the journey.

It helps to know how LPs think about the trajectory of a successful fund:

Real Money (Capital invested by LPs) → Not real money → Real Money (Capital returned to LPs)

(e.g. IRR, TVPI)

Being money managers, we have fancy labels for the different parts of this process. It's important to understand this language, but know that it's all just a bunch of words to try and articulate "HOW REAL THE MONEY IS." The only real money is the US dollars that get invested in the fund you are managing, and the money you distribute back.

Here are some examples of terms used to articulate money "REALness":

- **PIC** (paid-in capital): Real money invested at the start of the fund.

- **DPI** (distributions to paid-in): Real money returned to LPs. This is also known as the **realization multiple.** For example, if my LPs paid in $100M and I returned $2B, then DPI = 20.0.

- **TVPI** (total value to paid-in): Not real money. Refers to how much other people think your fund is worth. For example, if I've invested in one company and it's currently valued at 10x, then I can say my fund is worth 10.0 TVPI.

- **IRR** (internal rate of return): Not real money. Refers to the percentage of growth of the capital each year.

Until the startup exits and the money is returned to LPs, "gains" are imaginary, as far they're concerned. The startup might be valued at $10B by venture capitalists—but that money could still go up in smoke before the LPs see a dime in return. Realize that when you're talking to LPs about your portfolio pre-exit—when you're talking about

TVPI and IRR—you're talking about imaginary money and trying to make it feel real.

Become fluent in this language—make charts, share numbers—but don't get lost in it. VC isn't like other asset classes. It's not like private equity or real estate. There's a lot less liquidity, there's a lot more risk, and you can't do it from a spreadsheet. If later-stage fund managers are like scientists, then VCs are like artists. Your LPs know this. Don't try to be something you're not.

Entrepreneurs

One of my favorite questions to ask my grandfather is: "What's your favorite investment you ever made?"

I've asked this question dozens of times throughout our breakfasts, to see if there are new stories to unearth. But he always takes it back to the people he most enjoyed working with.

When you ask a good question of my grandfather, he'll sit and close his eyes for a second to collect his thoughts.

"I've worked with some amazing people," he says. "I helped the founders of Activision get going. But there was a great founder who left a big company to start his own. His name was Dave Bossen. His product had this way of controlling the water amount in paper. The company developed computer control systems for the paper industry."

Pops leans in to tell the rest of the story.

"You know why it was the best? Great people! And I got to travel all over the world for the board meetings!! One time, we went to Scotland and had the board meeting in a bar."

That company, Measurex, went public on the Nasdaq stock exchange in 1972 and was bought by Honeywell for $600m in the 1990s.

"I'm not a technologist, so I always trusted my network for understanding the technology," Pops says. "I've always been gifted with people and summing up the commitment and energy of the leadership."

Pops always says he looks for 3 things in founders:

- The energy to make it happen
- The commitment to see it through
- The integrity to build trust in the market

My list parallels his. I say "authenticity" where Pops says "integrity," but I think they go hand in hand. I agree that those are the raw textiles that make for a great entrepreneur.

Notice how "company hierarchy credentials" didn't make the list. Activision, which Pops backed in 1979, was founded by four game developers and a lawyer.

During their meeting at Sutter Hill, Pops asked the five of them, "Who's the CEO?"

The members of the Activision team all looked at one another. Then one of the developers looked at the lawyer and said, "Jim, you don't build anything—why don't you be the CEO?"

So, Jim became the CEO.

Those are the sort of people who build great companies. They're not like other people.

This is a good time to remember that **venture capital is a service job.** You serve entrepreneurs. You need to be there when things are on fire and when founders are complaining. You have to believe when no one else believes, including them.

Founders have enough judgment from their friends, family, and the broader market. They don't need more judgment from you. They're trying to find the people who can realize their dream of changing the world. You might be the perfect fit.

So, you need to pick those founders who make you feel excited and proud to serve them every day. Don't invest unless you enjoy the founders and want to hang out with these people for 10+ years.

Here are some of the questions I ask founders when I meet them for the first time:

Why are you doing this? If you're right, what does the world look like? What makes you the right person for this project? How does it make money? Why is this important? What's the most important thing to your business right now? What are your biggest roadblocks?

I also try to get them talking about something that has nothing to do with their business:

What's something you are proud of that you accomplished before the age of 21? What do you think about dinosaurs? What's the happiest place you've ever been?

As they're talking—about anything, from cartoons to cheeseburgers to basketball—I'm most often listening for two things:

1. Organic knowledge

2. The ability to default to movement

Organic knowledge is born of curiosity, following rabbit holes, and a drive to understand not only one topic, but the whole network of neighboring topics that might help you achieve goals in that area. It's distinct from artificial knowledge (the kind you get by following a prescribed syllabus in school). Founders with organic knowledge are able to clearly communicate the complexities of a subject to me. They have such an elite understanding of their market that they can articulate their unique insights with very little effort. It's something you hear in their voice.

The ability to **default to movement** is equally important: great leaders are thoughtful, but they live in motion. They're people of action, fundamentally. Anyone can entertain an idea. I do that all the time. Acting on those ideas, implementing them, executing a practical plan in the real world —those are things that come from being able to move, not just think.

To discern traits like energy, commitment, and authenticity, I'm constantly asking myself questions about founders. Here are some of the questions going through my head as I listen:

Energy

Can they communicate complex ideas? Am I captivated by the idea or person? Have they started a company before? (A repeat founder, even if failed, is preferred). Are they going to get distracted? Do they have the energy to maintain momentum for 10 years? Have they been punched in the face, and are they still moving forward? Something needs to power their battery through the years when there's no external validation or reward—what's their power source, and is it a strong enough reason to keep going? After the meeting, do I want to talk about them or their company with others?

Commitment

Is this more than a job to them? Are they committed to the mission? How committed are they (to themselves, their partners, and the mission)? At scale, does this matter? Is this a technology trying to find a problem, or is the problem clearly defined? Have they failed in the pursuit of this project before? (It's good if they have; it means they still want to see it through).

Authenticity

Do they have sufficient confidence in their own ability to solve problems, and/or in the mission of the company? Do they have any unique insights I haven't heard before? Do they have a unique insight about this specific market? Do they teach me something about the world? Are they consistent?

Finally, I think: **Does this person see the ball?**

I got the concept of "seeing the ball" from an outstanding baseball book called *The Mental Keys to Hitting*, by H.A. Dorfman (a famous baseball hitting coach). He writes:

"In dealing with the mental approach to hitting, a player must establish his priority—his core understanding of what's at the top of the list of requirements for being a skilled hitter. I've told countless professional players, 'However good your mechanics may be, you won't succeed if I blindfold you.' First things first: see the ball! 'Track it and whack it,' as I have often shouted from the dugout."

Pretty much exactly the same principle applies to founders. Their number-one priority, the thing they need to be doing "every waking hour," as Elon Musk once put it, is *seeing the ball.*

For a founder, this means:

- Talking and thinking about their business during every conversation, and in those conversations, listening to others' perspectives

- Late nights solving hard problems, with teams or alone

- Identifying the most important things to accomplish, and completing them (1 at a time)

- Talking to customers as often as possible

- Asking targeted people specific questions

- Sourcing potential customers all the time

- Staying up late and waking up early (more hours focused on the project increases the chances of success)

- Surrounding themselves with the right people for their quest

- Reading books purposefully—to get answers

- Exercising to keep their brains functioning

- Trying everything for the sake of the company

- Taking mistakes in stride, constantly moving forward (in the words of Thomas Edison: "I haven't failed; I've found 10,000 ways that won't work")

- Having a persistent fly in their ear, provoking radical action to solve the one problem they set out to solve

No individual item on this list constitutes seeing the ball, but these are the patterns.

I myself can't see the ball. As an investor, I get glimpses into moments of all these things, but I'm not at bat. So I'm looking for external signals that indicate they're seeing it.

Seeing the ball means knowing when you need to make a short-term sacrifice for the long-term success of the business. Part of it is knowing what the most important thing is today, so you can get to where you need to be next year.

For example:

- Coinbase founder Brian Armstrong spent almost 40% of his early funding on a legal letter that would allow Coinbase to get a bank account—

without it, they would never have gotten off the ground. Coinbase went public on the Nasdaq stock exchange in 2021 ($COIN)

- The Favor team (Ben Doherty and Zac Maurais) lived in every office they ever had. Favor was acquired by HEB Groceries for $180 million dollars.

- Talia Frenkel (Founder of ThisIsL) funded her first shipment of product with her savings as a photojournalist, and kept the company super lean to get to profitability. They were a team of 7 when acquired by P&G.

- Spenser Skates slept on a mattress on Curtis Liu's floor for a few months after moving from Chicago to found Amplitude—and for the following two years, they didn't pay themselves and lived off their savings. Amplitude went public on the Nasdaq Stock Exchange in 2021 ($AMPL).

All the best founders have similar stories of early and enduring commitment.

What's the most important thing today, for the long-term survival of the company? Founders who see the ball can answer this question.

In my experience, founders who see the ball are best equipped to attract the most dynamic people through three avenues: mission, product, and charisma. In crypto, especially early on, the people involved were driven chiefly by the mission. Many founders are builders at heart, and they rally people around their product because they love building useful things. And charisma is the ability to inspire. Great leaders inspire the team to persevere, and they also inspire customers to believe in what they're doing.

At the end of the day, a company is just an organism to attract the most capable people to further the founder's quest. If you really love the founder, do the deal. Even if you specialize in something else.

Co-founder Breakups

It's worth mentioning that not all founding partnerships are forever. Co-founder breakups happen. Sometimes, you might even see the possibility of a breakup when you first meet the founders. But that, by itself, shouldn't disqualify them in your eyes.

Co-founders who share the same values might still decide to go separate ways. It's a bummer, but it's okay. Sometimes the founding team that's perfect for year 1 isn't the right team to run the company in year 6. If at least one of the founders remains dedicated to the company, the company can survive a breakup.

The founders' ability to have these difficult conversations openly is the most important thing. Many difficult conversations happen during the life of a company. Some of the most difficult ones are related to the vision—as the founders try to figure out what this thing really is, at the core. Emotions are fine; name-calling isn't. What matters is that the founders can have difficult discussions peacefully, honestly and openly.

I find the best co-founders will debate almost violently about what the idea of "THE COMPANY" is, but they don't insult or harshly criticize each other. These relationships are built on a foundation of respect.

Chapter 4
LIFESTYLE

At Buck's, I asked the owner's son the secret to his success. His answer was perfect: "It's a lifestyle, not a job."

And just after he said this, he went and got a napkin to stop our table from rocking.

I hadn't even noticed the rocking.

In the VC lifestyle, you can also get a napkin to stop the table from rocking, metaphorically. You can spend time each day thinking about someone specific and what they need. I do this. Then you can connect them with the best resource you can find for whatever they need.

Here's how I visualize the VC lifestyle, as a virtuous cycle or flywheel with 3 parts:

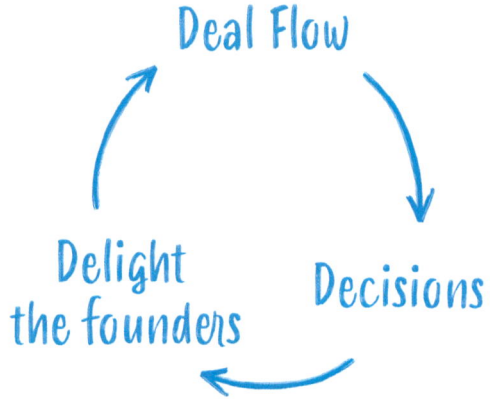

Having **deal flow** means you're able to find out about new companies, and get the opportunity to talk to them.

Once you have deal flow, you can make your **decisions** about which founders to support.

Once you've made those decisions, you need to **delight** those people. When you do that, it's like karma; your good reputation compounds, and you end up with more deal flow.

Pops made this lifestyle look effortless. It was second nature to him. He didn't just believe in the idea of delighting founders. He embodied his values.

For example, many times, someone would ask him a question during a meeting, and he'd say: "Oh, you have to talk to Jon Johnson about that!"

Right there in the meeting, he'd call Jon Johnson on the phone and say, "Hey Jon, I got this guy here who you should meet.

Do you have a minute?"

Then, he'd hand over the phone, let the person ask Jon the question, and forge that connection quickly. This is just a habit of his. I've done this a few times, but our generation doesn't have quite the same attitude toward phone calls. I often write intro emails for people during meetings, in the same spirit.

Of course, this only works if you're doing the work of building trust with all those people in your network all the time. That's how you can help people get what they're asking for (including funds from other VCs in your network).

You can't control whether that other investor will say yes, but you can stack the deck in a founder's favor by being a trustworthy filter.

The soul of venture is a desire to help people

get to where they want to go. Those people could be startups, LPs, other VCs... they can also just be humans you encounter along the way. Finding energy in giving that assistance will power your battery through this job.

The job becomes a lifestyle once you've chosen to make it part of your identity. Personally, I often say "I'm a deal junkie." That's just who I am. I always want to make deals with people. I try to identify the most important things and people, and make deals happen around those things and those people. This matters because when people make good deals, everyone's better off. Think of how many deals Amazon facilitates each day and how much better off we all are because of it!

A decade into this lifestyle, I'm still learning every day.

Chapter 5
TRUST

In his book, *The Startup Game*, Pops wrote:

"Wise venture capitalists—the ones who earn a solid reputation—are used to working on a handshake. They willingly share the ever-present risk of failure and are not in it for quick gain through stock flipping. These individuals are careful, because each investment should have the potential to lead to a long-term, successful relationship. They are also careful because their reputation is

inextricably tied to each company they back. Any company may fail, and many do. In and of itself, that is not a big deal. But how should venture capitalists behave in the wake of that failure? Are they calm and consistent in good times and bad? Is their advice helpful? Are their contacts useful? Do they follow through on their commitments? If they don't get consistently good grades in all of these areas, they won't last long in what is a surprisingly tight-knit community."

When my grandfather's friend George Shultz turned 100, he wrote that the most important lesson he learned was: "Trust is the coin of the realm."

This should be the mantra of all VCs. Magic happens when trust is highest.

Being trustworthy means *your word is your bond*. This is true for both investors and entrepreneurs, and it's essential to all good relationships.

One of my favorite parts of having breakfast with my grandfather is the respect he gives others. Continuing to eat at Buck's, week after week, year after year, is one small, iterative way to build trust. Everyone knows him by name. The same waiters fight to wait on him, and they'll give him his pick of tables every time we walk in.

This is a massive topic that we could talk about until the end of time. Here are a few notes on how it appears in VC:

- You can't fake trust. It's about being true to your own personal set of values, every day. It's about saying what you're going to do and doing it—enough times that people believe it will always happen. Trust is the long game.

- I have seen many investors come and go, breaking the rule of trust. They're flashes in the pan. The best VCs are built for endurance.

- It's about keeping the promises you've made to yourself as much as to others. Pops would always say, "Let's make both sides of the table happy." Soon enough, people learned they could trust him to actually do that. That's how he was able to do thousands of deals over the course of his life, and how he was able to keep doing deals until he was 95 (and he still does deals).

- We have a rule at Boost VC: Compound trust. Get rich slowly. Long, slow money is the game, and it comes from compounding trust. You're not compounding money. You're compounding trust. Because of that trust, you will be welcomed. When you have that trust everywhere you go, you will be unbeatable in our business because people know they can depend on you. You are delivering on the promise that you will work hard on the companies, be there for the companies, and spend time on the companies. You don't have to be right all the time. You only have to be right once or twice, but you always have to be trustworthy. That's how this business is.

- Build trust through mutual experience.

- Give trust to people who haven't earned it yet. Give them the chance to earn it.

- Trust isn't a flash in the pan. You can commit overnight, but you can't build trust overnight. People often say things like "look at that founder who raised $25M in 2 weeks!" But they did NOT raise $25M in 2 weeks. They raised $25M over 5 years, and it looks like 2 weeks because the trust had already been built over 5 years. My grandfather has always known this.

- Broadly, trust allows you to move more quickly through deals and workflows.

- Stay true to your word. Founders need to trust you to stay true to your word.

- If you say you're going to do a deal, do the deal.

- Your LPs need to trust you to not run away with their money.

- Your founders need to have the integrity to build trust in the market. And in order to scale, founders need to trust the people on their teams to be better than they are at everything.

It's human nature that people will live up to the trust you give them. If you invest money and say, "I believe in you, and I think you will make this company an incredible success," you're showing your trust, and the entrepreneur will do whatever she/he can to prove you right.

On the other hand, if you hold the money and say, "You better not blow this," you're telling the entrepreneur that you don't trust them. That can become a self-fulfilling prophecy: they may end up being untrustworthy because they don't get a good trusting vibe from you, and you don't get it from them.

The job itself is so simple. You raise capital from people with money; you invest in founders who require money; you return more capital than you raised. That's the job. But these are big bets, and there's a lot on the line.

It's about more than money—it's about the actualization of human endeavor; it's about how the world's most brilliant people spend their precious time; it's about whether people in the future will live better lives than ours. That's why trust is more valuable than money.

Chapter 6
CONVICTION

In VC, you're paid to make decisions. At least once per fund, one of those decisions needs to be right. Conviction is the root of those decisions. This is one point of real consensus in the Draper family.

Pops proposed to my grandmother, Phyllis, after 3 days. Talk about conviction! He was on a cruise ship at the time. He'd recently returned from the Korean War, where he'd narrowly, very luckily avoided dying. He wasn't about to waste any time moving forward with his life. Interestingly, Phyllis wasn't supposed to be on the market. She was wearing another man's engagement ring; her fiancé just wasn't on the boat. That didn't matter to Pops. He proposed anyway. It worked out; my grandmother stayed with Pops for the rest of her life.

High-conviction decisions usually have some friction. The world will present obstacles, often via the people you respect the most. When I was going all-in on Bitcoin, my grandfather told me that I "shouldn't be the first Draper to go to jail"... so, naturally, I did it anyway.

I see conviction in VC as *the strong belief that _____ won't stop growing.* **This company** won't stop growing, **this market** won't stop growing, **these people** won't stop growing.

You build this conviction over time. Years into your business relationship, you still believe in the founders and the founding team. The big goal is to build such enduring conviction that *you'll never want to sell this asset.* The whole job is predicated on finding those companies that you'll never want to sell (and the people who run them) because of who they are, because of the people who work with them, and because of the mission they're on.

Pops phrased it this way: "Sometimes you think you want to sell something because the price seems high, and you're worried that it might go down. Remember why you invested in the first place. If none of those things have changed, then you shouldn't sell unless you need the money. And even then, you're never sad if you sell half."

In the 1950s Pops believed the technology industry wouldn't stop growing. He learned all about this new industry, established a firm belief in that industry, and invested based on that. He built conviction, kept making decisions based on that conviction, and kept deepening his conviction over the course of his career. He spent as much time as possible with the people who were putting in the blood, sweat, and tears in that thesis area, which he believed was undervalued and misunderstood, and he kept reinforcing the core decisions he'd already made.

One of the hardest things in VC is sustaining your conviction (and not doubting yourself). Your windfalls are big, few, and far between. You'll feel tempted to re-make decisions. A little voice in your head will say things like, "Well, I already made that decision, so I

should be making new decisions." You'll feel tempted to change your mind and try making more bets based on different decisions.
But the best approach is to make a small number of decisions—and use those as the foundation for many others. I wish I'd realized this sooner than I did.

Humans always want to create new decisions for themselves. But the best investors know that if they were right about something, then they don't start being wrong about it! Sometimes you should look at your portfolio and just say, "Hey, instead of making a new decision—that old decision is crushing it. Let's double down."

Enduring conviction is the trophy you get at the end of a decade of early investments. Warren Buffett is amazing as this. He knew from the beginning that investing wasn't a one-time decision: you build up your ownership over time.

My Conviction about Bitcoin

My biggest high-conviction move to date was going all-in on Bitcoin. At that time, in 2011, the entire sector was called "the Bitcoin space"—there were no other notable cryptocurrencies.

Boost VC became the first fund to focus on founders building in that category. Since then, we've supported more than 100 crypto companies through Boost VC, including Etherscan, Wyre, Unstoppable Domains, Keep, Ripio, Aragon, Polychain, and many others.

It started with a stroke of luck: I met Brian Armstrong; he pitched me Coinbase and sparked my interest in Bitcoin. Sitting across from me at Red Rock Coffee, he said: "Someday the world will be on one financial infrastructure. I believe Bitcoin is that infrastructure, and Coinbase is the gateway."

I didn't invest then and there. I followed the trail of breadcrumbs that Brian started me on, exploring the industry and the people whose blood, sweat, and tears were all over it. Wow! What a world!

After that legwork, I had only a few days left to make my decision about Coinbase. The moment that tipped the scales happened when I was sitting on the toilet. Absentmindedly, I started flipping through an issue of *The Economist* that had been lying beside my toilet for a year and a half. I saw a headline—something like "Is the

Bitcoin Bubble Bursting?"—and I thought "That's crazy. This magazine has been here for a year and a half. But I'm here now, thinking about Bitcoin, weighing the idea of investing in Coinbase."

I became convinced that "the Bitcoin space" wouldn't stop growing.

That night, I called Brian and said I was ready to invest. That was the best investment I've made so far. But I should have taken my conviction even further than that. The day the Coinbase wire came through, Brian called to thank me for investing and to get me amped up (a smooth move for any founder). In that same call, he said, "Other investors are matching their investment in Coinbase, putting the same amount of money into Bitcoin."

In my head, I'm like—*you gotta be kidding me, man, I just gave you a bunch of money, and now you want MORE money??*

So I didn't do it, but I wish I had. That would've been an even better investment than Coinbase.

Hot Takes

Often, the best investments come from the loudest debates among partners. Founders will present a counter-intuitive or contrarian concept; someone will LOVE it, and someone else will HATE it. Those are the startups striking a nerve. Those are the startups doing something IMPORTANT!

Good investors have hot takes about when conventional wisdom is wrong, and that unlocks the potential for conviction in unconventional ideas.

- Imagine investing in Uber when conventional wisdom said, "Don't get into a stranger's car."

- Imagine investing in video games when conventional wisdom said, "Being good at video games makes you dumber and less appealing to colleges."

- Imagine investing in SpaceX when only the government was allowed to make rockets.

- Imagine investing in Tesla when the best electric car was a golf cart that could only run for an hour on a charge.

- With Benchling, the conventional wisdom was, "The life sciences industry won't adopt new technologies."

- With Plangrid, it was the same thing: "The construction industry is too big and slow to move over to software; it's all pen and paper."

- I invested in Bitcoin when only governments were allowed to issue currency. It's not that I liked fintech —I didn't. I liked the rebellion against the legacy system.

Early stage investment often takes understanding when conventional wisdom splits from the truth.

The ability to see these unconventional points of view is so important that we've been experimenting with ways to test for it during our interview process at Boost. When we were hiring our first associate, I bought him a box of sports cards and said, "Find me the 15 best cards in this box."

That night, he went through all the cards, sorted them, and made a presentation of the 15 best cards. He said, "These 5 are the obvious best. These 5 are the next tier down. And these 5 are my hot takes."

I asked him about one of his hot takes: a quarterback most people would've ignored completely. He said, "I watched him in college. This guy's explosive and dynamic, the way most people aren't. He'll be an enduring player. He'll be awesome."

This maps to venture. You don't invest purely based on your hot take, but if you don't have a hot take, you probably won't invest. The founders you want aren't the obvious best. They aren't the next tier down from being the obvious best, either. They're undervalued. It takes an eagle-eyed talent scout to spot them. Those are the bets you're trying to make.

Think about it logically for a second. If the idea was an obvious "GOOD IDEA," it should've been funded by the government, big corporations, or one of the biggest venture capital funds.

The earlier you are in your early-stage venture career, the less likely you are to see the **obvious** best or second-best. You're going to see the leftovers of the leftovers—the people who haven't gotten support from the massive VC firms like Sequoia and A16Z, from FAANG companies, or from the government. You're at the bottom of the food chain fielding the little guys. But that's where the most lucrative returns are, those are the companies that change the world. The companies no one sees coming. You're looking for the leftovers of the leftovers that just might change the world. They need your belief!

Chapter 7
LUCK

One morning while we were verbally sparring with each other, Pops and I landed on the topic of luck and venture capital. Between bites of eggs and bacon, he said, "Life has a way of presenting you with luck. The people who take it are the people who succeed."

More than any other Pops quote, this is the line I say to people nearly every day.

What if my grandfather had chosen not to take his first venture capital job? Before going into venture, Pops was working at Inland Steel and living in Indiana. He was a rising star there—on track to become the apex predator in its corporate hierarchy. When his dad called him and asked for help with some weird business in California, he could have said no.

This was a doorway to an opportunity with unknown upside, and instead of acting fearfully, he went for it. The luckiest people just go for it.

When he turned in his resignation, the president of Inland Steel yelled at him for two hours for even thinking this was a good idea. Many other people shared the president's opinion that Pops was walking away from the best opportunities he would ever get.

As Pops told me this story, he said he remembered thinking: *This is the best decision I've ever made, because this is the most I've ever been yelled at in my life!*

He smiled at me, then quickly followed up with: "I want some more maple syrup."

The topic of luck comes up quite a bit during our conversations. On this particular day the topic had been brought up, I was referring to the luck of picking a great startup.

Early stage venture capital is a unique business—and I do mean unique. It's difficult to attribute your successes to great skill OR great luck. The time frame of success is a decade. It takes 10 years to see if you're right or wrong. A lot happens in that time.

If you ever have the luxury of looking back on your investment in one of the most world-changing companies, just remember that we're in the service business. We were lucky to be a part of the founder's journey.

I believe the danger of this business is in looking back and believing you were smart. Sometimes you were smart; sometimes you weren't. But you were lucky either way.

Celebrating the Coinbase IPO with Pops

Chapter 8
THINGS I SAY TO FOUNDERS

Most of *Breakfast With Pops* has been addressed to other VCs and aspiring VCs—not to founders. That's because a good investor avoids telling founders how to do their jobs. But there are a handful of things I say to founders. Here they are.

- "A lot of entrepreneurs make the mistake of protecting the board from bad news. If you don't remember anything else I've said, remember this: get the bad news out fast." — Pops

- "The chairman of the board probably should not be you. It should be somebody you can talk to over lunch in a tough situation." — Pops

- Perfect is the enemy of done.

- You will eventually need to stop "doing everything." In the early days of a startup, especially for first-time founders, there's self-confidence in understanding everything that goes on under the hood of your company. The early days are when you establish your obsession, and begin building your seedling brand. You take pride in the "doing everything" mentality. However, championships are won by teams, not individuals. In order to scale yourself, you have to trust the people on your team to be better than you at doing everything. They should be All Stars who challenge you.

- Someone out there loves doing the job you suck at.

- Seek criticism rather than fighting it.

- Be thoughtful, but default to movement.

- VCs are NOT your customers.

- Product-market fit is a kid selling ice-cold lemonade on the hottest day of summer. Everyone who stops at the lemonade stand has 2 things in common: (1) they're supporting someone they think is worth supporting, and (2) they want the damn lemonade. When you have product-market fit, you're providing something people need, not what you thought they needed.

- Finally: **Be the cockroach!** That's our motto at Boost. It's one of the first things I see every time I walk into our office.

"Be the cockroach" came from a startup called Favor. They were in the crowded market of the on-demand food delivery space, but carved out their own space outside of California and made their way to a good exit.

However, before they had any semblance of success, they lived in every office they ever had and ran out of money twice; also, every time we connected with them, we weren't sure if they were headed in the right direction.

But we always ended up saying—"But they won't die," and we started calling them cockroaches. Then, we realized they took *pride* in being cockroaches.

Ben Doherty, one of the co-founders, said, "Yeah! We're like cockroaches. The funny thing about cockroaches is they're really hard to kill, and no one likes them in their space."

And suddenly, we took pride in calling our companies cockroaches. We defined a cockroach as a resourceful startup that survives no matter what. The competition ignores them, yet fears they'll enter their space. They're awake day and night. They're quick, agile, and good at adapting to their environment.

Come what may on planet Earth, one thing that won't change is the nature of cockroaches. The nature of great entrepreneurs is similarly unchanging. And wherever they exist, there will be people like Pops, my dad, me, and maybe you, who love to see them win against all odds.

Glossary of Startup Lingo

Assembled by Chris Kauzmann and Lisa Getzler

Acquisition: one company buys most or all of another company's shares to gain control of that company.

Angel Investor: a high-net-worth individual or networked group of individuals who provide (via their own money) financial backing for small startups or entrepreneurs, typically in an early pre-seed or seed round in exchange for equity ownership in the company.

API: application programming interface (API). A set of programming codes used to query data, parse responses, and send instructions between one software platform and another.

Blockchain: a digital system of recording information. A blockchain is essentially a digital ledger of transactions that is duplicated and distributed across the entire network of computer systems on the blockchain. This distributed structure makes it difficult to change, hack, or cheat the system. Blockchains are best known for their crucial role in cryptocurrency systems.

Blue Ocean: an entrepreneurship industry term used to describe a new market with little competition or few barriers. In contrast to a "red ocean," a blue ocean isn't already saturated with participants. It's full of opportunities for innovation.

Bootstrapping: starting a company with little capital, relying on money other than outside investments.

Business to Business (B2B): the term B2B may describe a business, product, service, or transaction. It means business is being conducted between companies, rather than between a company and individual consumers.

Business to Consumer (B2C): the term B2C may describe a business, product, service, or transaction. It means products and services are being sold by a business to individual consumers (not to other businesses).

Burn Rate: the rate at which a new company is spending venture capital (typically) to finance its overhead before generating positive cash flow.

Convertible Note: short-term debt that converts into equity.

Cliff Vesting: the process by which employees earn the right to receive prescribed benefits (equity, retirement contributions, etc.) from their company at a specified date, rather than becoming vested gradually over a period of time.

Crowdfunding: the use of small amounts of capital from a large number of individuals to finance a new business venture or project.

Cryptocurrency: a digital or virtual currency (e.g. Bitcoin) that is secured by cryptography based on blockchain technology, which makes it nearly impossible to counterfeit or double-spend.

Customer Discovery: the initial and iterative process of understanding customers' situations, needs, and pain points.

Deck or Pitch Deck: a slide presentation used by a founder when pitching to investors.

Dilution: a decrease in existing stockholders' ownership percentage of a company that occurs when the company issues new shares.

Disruptive Technology: an innovation that significantly alters the way that consumers, industries, or businesses operate.

Due Diligence: an investigation of a potential investment (such as a startup) to confirm all facts. For example, investors might look at financial records, interview customers, and explore other indicators of a company's performance.

Equity: the amount of money that would be returned to a company's shareholders if all of the assets were liquidated (and all of the company's debt was paid off).

Exit Event: occurs when the owners of a company "exit" the business by selling it. Exit events can take the form of an Initial Public Offering (IPO), acquisition, or selling shares.

Follow-on Funding: additional funding for a firm following the initial investment made by investors. Firms that qualify typically obtain their money in stages that correspond to their stage of development. Once a venture capitalist makes an investment in a firm, subsequent investments are made in rounds (or stages) and are referred to as follow-on funding.

Fiat Money: a government-issued currency that is not backed by a physical commodity, such as gold or silver, but rather by the government that issued it.

Friends and Family Round: funding that allows a startup to get through its first few months of operation (typically $10,000 to $150,000). The funding comes from friends, family, and personal connections, rather than an accredited investor. This is one way in which founders "bootstrap."

Gas Fees: the fee, or pricing value, required to successfully conduct a transaction or execute a contract on the Ethereum blockchain platform.

EBITDA: earnings before interest, taxes, depreciation, and amortization. This is a measure of a company's overall financial performance and is sometimes used as an alternative to net income.

Incubator: an organization engaged in the business of fostering early-stage companies through the different developmental phases until the companies have sufficient financial, human, and physical resources to function on their own.

Intellectual Property (IP): an umbrella term for a set of intangible assets such as inventions and designs. Intellectual property is owned by a company or individual and can be legally protected via patents & copyrights to prevent outside use or implementation without consent or compensation.

Initial Public Offering (IPO): An initial public offering or stock launch is a public offering via a stock exchange, like the Nasdaq or NYSE, in which shares of a company are sold to institutional investors and usually also retail investors.

Key Performance Indicators (KPIs): the measurable outcomes of business decisions that leaders specify as necessary to continue running and resourcing a company, product or service.

Lifestyle Business: a business set up and run by its founders primarily with the aim of sustaining a particular level of income and no more. Such companies may be multi-million dollar companies in terms of revenue or equity. However, they tend to be self-limiting in their ability to expand and are not designed for scale. They tend to be focused on one or more key persons, the loss of whom will stop the company in its tracks.

Metaverse: a digital reality that combines aspects of social media, online gaming, augmented reality (AR), virtual reality (VR), and cryptocurrencies to allow users to interact virtually.

Minimum Viable Product (MVP): a product with enough features to attract early-adopter customers and validate a product idea early in the product development cycle.

Mining: a process by which new bitcoins are entered into circulation. Mining is also the way that new transactions are confirmed by the network and a critical component of the maintenance and development of the blockchain ledger. It is performed using sophisticated hardware that solves an extremely complex computational math problems.

Non-Fungible Tokens (NFTs): cryptographic assets on a blockchain with unique identification codes and metadata that distinguish them from each other.

Post-Money Valuation: a company's estimated worth after outside financing and/or capital injections are added to its balance sheet.

Pre-Money Valuation: a company's estimated worth before it goes public or receives new investments.

Product-Market Fit: the alignment between customers' specific problem/need/desire and the solution a business has created for them.

Return on Investment (ROI): A performance measure used to evaluate the efficiency or profitability of an investment or compare the efficiency of a number of different investments. ROI tries to directly measure the amount of money made on a particular investment, relative to the investment's cost.

SAFE Note: SAFE (or Simple Agreement for Future Equity) notes are documents that startups often use when raising seed capital. Essentially, a SAFE note acts as a legally binding promise to allow an investor to purchase a specified number of shares for an agreed-upon price at some point in the future.

Seed Funding: the type of financing used in the formation of a startup. Funding is provided by private investors—usually in exchange for an equity stake in the company or for a share in the profits of a product.

Series A, B, C, etc.: after startups raise "seed" funding or angel investor funding at the outset, they may raise more money during funding "rounds" that are called Series A, Series B, Series C, etc. These are necessary ingredients for a business that decides bootstrapping, or merely surviving off of the generosity of friends, family and the depth of their own pockets, will not suffice.

Software as a Service (SaaS): a software licensing model in which access to the software is provided on a subscription basis.

Special Purpose Acquisition Company (SPAC): a company without commercial operations that is formed strictly to raise capital through an initial public offering (IPO) for the purpose of acquiring or merging with an existing company.

Term Sheet: a non-binding agreement that shows the basic terms and conditions of an investment.

Unicorn: an industry term used to describe a privately held startup company with a value of over $1 billion.

Venture Capital (VC): a type of private equity financing in which professionally managed investment funds are provided to startup companies in exchange for some amount of negotiated ownership in the company. Appropriate for startups that are predicted to have long-term growth potential and a profitable exit.

Venture Debt: a type of financing that some startup companies seek, typically provided in the form of a loan. Unlike equity financing, venture debt doesn't typically involve giving up ownership in the company.

Vesting: a legal term that refers to the point in time when the rights and interests arising from legal ownership of a company are acquired by an employee. A vesting schedule is an incentive program for employees that gives them benefits, usually stock options, after they have worked at a company for a specified period of time.

Thanks for reading.

Please send feedback (and deals!) to:

adam@boost.vc

Credits

Written by:
Adam Draper
William Henry Draper, III

Directed by:
Sam Nightengale

Produced by:
Altamira Studio

Edited by:
Ellen Fishbein

Designed by:
Pilar Keprta
Sam Nightengale

Printed by:
Texas Bindery

Special thanks:

Jean Am	Erik Franks
Alex Bailey	Kevin G.
Phil Becker	Ben Gilbert
Ann Marie Benitez	Brandon Goldman
Wayne Benitez	Matthew Gould
Alex Case	Matt "Gundy" Gunderson
Greg Castle	Joyce Guo
Danny Cotter	Max Haot
Gabriella Covino	Baha Hariri
Emmanuel de Maistre	Emma Harrelson
Gus Domel	Nick Healy
Andrea Draper	Rachel Huh
Timothy Draper	Brad Kam
Scott Edwards	Shamez Kanji
Gabe Finnell	Mitchell Katz
Thomas Foley	Chris Kauzmann

Rish Kumar

Fernanda Lazarte

Collin McDonnell

Josh Miller

Skyler Mott

Carol Obando-Derstine

Peter Pastewka

Annie Pearl

David Pearl

Anthony Pompliano

Gabriel Richardson

Jorge Richardson

Jessica Robertson

Ella Rossetti

Adam Schouela

Fark Tari

Kevin Twohy

James Walker

Collin West

Brayton Williams

Marcus Yco

Chen Zhang

www.altamira.studio